Exit the Labyrinth

A Journey Back to Yourself

Rimu Bhattarai

Exit the Labyrinth

Exit the Labyrinth

"The darker the night, the brighter the stars."
— Fyodor Dostoevsky, Crime and Punishment

Exit the Labyrinth

*To everyone that is still stuck in the darkness, remember
there is always a way out.*

I hope to meet you there.

Table of Contents

Prologue

I wrote this book for the quiet little girl that couldn't speak her truth. I wrote it because I am sick and tired of keeping her secrets, even now that she is long gone. I made a promise to her many years ago that her story would not go untold. That I would make sure the world would hear her words, even if she could not speak them herself. I share these pieces with you for all the little girls and boys out there that are still hiding their truth. For all those still keeping those secrets buried beneath layers of themselves, kept locked away from the world and even their own minds. It is time for us to rise and to speak our truth. Make sure that it is known.

Most of us spend our lives attempting to repress the emotions and memories of the darkest points of our existence. What happened to us was not okay. The trauma, the abuse, whatever it may be differs for each of us, but we are the chosen ones. We have survived against all odds. It is now our job to make sure that whatever happened to us never happens again, not to anyone.

As a species, we keep repeating the same karmic cycles of toxicity. For too long people have spread the hatred that they were shown, kicking the can to the next person so they don't have to deal with the issues in front of them. It has to come to an end. People must be held accountable for what they've done. Even if they can't feel our pain, let them read about it. Let them hear our stories. And let the world know that we will no longer stay silent.

My name is Rimu, and this is my story. A story of hope. My journey to the path of peace. My fight for not only survival, but something worth surviving for: life, and all of the joys that come with it. And though I have yet to see what is on the other side, there is peace in my mind knowing that whatever is waiting for me is worth living for.

What is a Labyrinth?

A labyrinth is an intricate structure designed for you to immerse yourself in. Its pathway leads you to a center point and back out again. Unlike a maze that has many different routes you can take, a labyrinth has one singular path. Though they both only have one way out. Trapped in a maze, you can easily spend forever going in the wrong direction. You won't know if you've made the wrong decision until you hit a wall. You only know if you've made the right decisions once you find your way out. In a labyrinth there is no wrong answer. There is only in and out.

The healing journey is a labyrinth. In our youth, the world takes our genes and our experiences and molds us into one version of ourselves. The more we experience, the more that mold changes. It is inevitable that one day some catalytic event occurs that causes that mold to shatter. The identity that we formed is gone. That is when we are presented with the labyrinth: a journey back to ourselves.

In order to find our way back to ourselves, we must first lose ourselves. Trauma is complex and has numerous side effects. After we experience something life altering, we are left with this darkness inside of ourselves, something we've never seen before. And if we aren't equipped with the right tools to process what has happened, which we are most often not, the darkness inside of us begins to grow. Before we realize it, we are grasping for anything to keep it away —and somehow that is what leads us straight into its arms. Everything we once knew is crumbling before us, and there is nothing left to hold on to. So we wander aimlessly down the pathway to the abyss. And though the path only leads forward, forward is headed down.

Reshaping ourselves requires not only deciding who we want to be, but also learning — through experience — who we don't want to be. We begin to make choices that would frighten the past version of ourselves, the versions of ourselves that are dead and gone. We end up in karmic cycles, spreading toxicity with others that are stuck in the same darkness. We continue this cycle until we eventually, hopefully, begin to realize that the problems in our lives are a reflection of what is inside of us. This is the realization we make when we hit the center of the labyrinth. We are then faced with a decision: do we stay and rot in this dark place, or do we move forward and make our way out?

Chapter I: The Abyss

"Whoever fights monsters should see to it that in the process he does not become a monster. And if you gaze long enough into an abyss, the abyss will gaze back into you."
—Friedrich Nietzsche

Exit the Labyrinth

Trauma is darkness that is palpable. Not simply the lack of light that we are all familiar with. Rather, it is the shadowy figure lurking in the corner of your bedroom, the monster that hides under the bed. It patiently waits for you to be at your most vulnerable, until you are blissfully asleep, to torment you in your dreams. It is the monster we must all face and is different for each of us. No one's experience is the same and the demons that result are a mere reflection of whatever horrors we each have encountered.

The abyss is where we go when we experience trauma. It is a dark hole that exists in each of us. There we lay, buried deep in the graves of our past selves. The darkness seems eternal and the demons inside of us feed off of it. The more we ignore it, the more we let that darkness fester. The darkness transforms into a poison. And the longer we avoid dealing with our trauma, the more the poison spreads. The poison roots give birth to poisoned fruit. Before you know it, it soils everything else around you. Everything becomes tainted with the darkness and eventually it begins to rot.

The demons thrive on the darkness, the poison. They grow bigger and stronger while the light inside of us slowly fades away, until there is nothing left. As the light in us fades we begin to turn into the monsters we've been running from. We sink deeper and deeper into the abyss and begin to develop vices to try and escape from the darkness. We become willing to do anything in our power to hide from the reflection in the mirror, to avoid facing who we are and what we have become as a result of our trauma.

We become a product of our environment. The woeful result of unfortunate circumstances. As we get sucked deeper into the abyss, we begin to morph into the very monsters that kept us up at night. The world goes from black and white into varying shades of gray we never could have imagined possible, as we become no better than our worst enemies. We all have secrets to hide, memories we are ashamed of. Excuses to stay in the darkness. And until we are brave enough to face it, we do. We let ourselves tumble down the rabbit hole through the abyss.

Though I have crafted these poems and stories with pretty words and metaphors —make no mistake of this— there is nothing glamorous about this type of darkness. It took everything I had to make it out alive, but I am still missing chunks of flesh and I may never become whole again. I share these with you in hopes that you too will see that no matter how dark it gets, there is always a way out, even though the only way out is through.

Welcome to my abyss.

Exit the Labyrinth

Choking on syllables

Words turn to ash in my mouth

So vulgar

I had to spit them out:

-the truth

Exit the Labyrinth

Blood flows red

Scars run deep

I'm drowning under the weight

Of the secrets I keep

-I guess blood isn't thick enough

Exit the Labyrinth

The devil isn't lurking under your bed
Monsters are known to live inside of men.
Until the day comes when you look one in the eye
You'll never truly know whether the soul is dead
or alive.

-monsters and men

Exit the Labyrinth

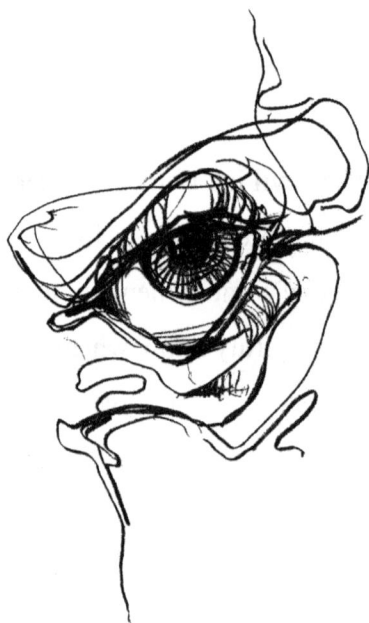

Exit the Labyrinth

I wish this poem was about a boy
One with glacier eyes or tangles of curly hair
But the truth is
This dark tale is about you
And all of the pain you put me through.

Years of pain and torture
Gaslighting me for putting up boundaries
You made a fool out of me.
Doing anything to keep me quiet
Your blanket of darkness trying to bury me silent.

I wish this poem was about a boy
One that was mean, that would lie or cheat
But it was you
Too rough with my body
A corrupted vision
Reenacting your twisted fantasies
You chewed me up and spit me out
I still remember the taste of poison in my mouth.

I wish this poem was about a boy
But they say blood runs thicker than water
And three things can't be hidden for long

Exit the Labyrinth

The sun, the moon, and the truth.
Your secret lays heavy on my shoulders
But I can't hold its weight forever
Even if I keep my mouth shut
I know it will find its way back to you.
-my name is Rimu and I am not afraid

Exit the Labyrinth

Calloused hands

Travel over soft skin

What an odd piece of candy

It tastes nothing like strawberries.

This is so vile

I think as my mouth fills with bile.

I gag.

I choke.

My knees are so *cold.*

Don't bite.

Don't scream.

I feel so *unclean.*

I can't wait to go to bed tonight

So I can silently scream until light.

-hard rotten candy

Exit the Labyrinth

Am I your prize?

The cherry on top of a sundae

We both know you already took mine

Plucked before it ripened.

Your little Lolita

I've always been your favorite crime

Your shiny trophy

That you'll forever hide.

-I may be the prize, but you'll never be a winner

Exit the Labyrinth

Your ignorant words

Brush up against my ear

A whisper with the wind

Sounds I don't wish to hear

You see,

Intuition differs from fear

For one makes us certain

The other one draws tears

And you should never listen

To someone who knows neither.

-ignorance

Exit the Labyrinth

Stuck beneath your shadow,

You taught me how to live in it

So that I would never be able to see the sun

And become it myself.

The truth is, you've always lived in fear

Knowing the light that lives within me

Shines brighter

Than yours ever could.

-dimmed

Exit the Labyrinth

I try to run and hide

But there you are

Two steps ahead of me each time

Blocking every corner

Until there's no other way forward.

You disappear, sly as ever

But I feel your presence

Slowly creeping up behind me

Looming in the shadows

And feeding on my darkness

Growing stronger and stronger

Until I cannot ignore you any longer

-*my trauma*

Exit the Labyrinth

You think it's been long enough
You think I've forgotten
All the hatred you once showed me
All those secrets I've been keeping
No longer!
Just wait until the world sees
All the damage you have done to me
Who will you be then?
When the mask comes off
Revealing the wicked face
You've been hiding for so long.
It's time the people see
The monster you are
For you haven't changed
And I'll never lose my scars.

-memories I'll never forget (again)

Exit the Labyrinth

Your body once bloomed with fire

Now drowned from its light

The fly of death came to collect its debt

In the middle of the night.

I can't help but stare

As it circles around your corpse

Like you were never even there.

It buzzes so softly

Trying to enter your open mouth

No one bothered to shut it

So it flys in and out.

I want to scream

And swat it away

But I'm stuck standing still

While you're turning grey.

-the fly of death

Exit the Labyrinth

Your sharp words erupt fissures down my wrists
Blood and violence leak all over the bathroom
sink
The music blaring in my headphones doesn't
drown out the screaming
My mother's broken sobs have lost their meaning.
It went from every weekend to every evening
No amount of pain can distract me from what I'm
feeling.

I fantasize about the day I leave this fractured
house
Abandon my life here and move somewhere far
down south
But for now I'll sit on the floor, my hand covering
my mouth
Choking on tears because there's no way out.
-*broken home/shattered hope*

Exit the Labyrinth

How is it
I got so tangled

In your cleverly woven

Web of lies?

Thank goodness

For that pretty face of yours

You seem to have everyone fooled

But it's only a matter of time

Until someone spills the truth

About the monster lurking beneath

Your lovely suit of skin.

-black widow

Exit the Labyrinth

I'm sorry I don't want to watch
You live your new bodacious life
After you spent so much of it
Trying to destroy the potential of mine.
My entire childhood spent
In the wicked fantasies of your mind
A horror film with you as the star
Imaginary world of nightmares come to life.
Never the lead, always the backup
In your showcase you found delight
You always found your ecstasy
Watching the terror in my eyes.
Were you just a girl,
Or a creature of the night?
Gaining all of your power
Bleeding out the light in mine.
I hope it was worth it
Now that you've lost me in this life
I'm not the little girl you remember
For now I'm full of spite.
-the ugly truth

Exit the Labyrinth

Icy hands

Can't warm the devil inside

As you try and rip out

The God in mine

-these hands belong to no God, only the devil

Exit the Labyrinth

Searing pain shoots down my spine

I drop to my knees

Paralyzed, I can't move, can't speak

The traitor moves to sight

And my jaw drops at who I see

A bloody knife in your hands

Tainting every memory

-betrayal

Exit the Labyrinth

They say a woman's hands

Are more gentle than a man's

But in my experience

They're just as rough.

You think they would be softer

To the touch

Yet I've found they wander

Just as much.

-evil comes in all forms

Exit the Labyrinth

Chapter II: Me vs. My Mind

*"Men are not prisoners of fate, but only prisoners
of their own minds"*
-—Franklin D. Roosevelt

Exit the Labyrinth

As I began to slip into the darkness, my mind turned volatile. My one safe place I had in the world vanished. The place I had once relied on, the only escape I had, was now brimming with anxious thoughts that would never stay away. Slowly but surely this began to chip away at my wellbeing. Endless sleepless nights resulted in permanent dark circles under my eyes. I looked like the corpse I was inside. Dead. Lifeless. And waiting for the day I truly became so.

It took a long time for my mind to quieten down, but things got a lot worse before that happened.

Exit the Labyrinth

She was not bright
Like the scorching sun in the sky
Instead she moved with the shadows
A slave to the darkness of night
Waiting for the day
She perished in the light.
-ruled by the moon

Exit the Labyrinth

Another sleepless night dissolved
All hope of rest lost
In the battle of my mind
My memories won.
-sleepless nights

Exit the Labyrinth

What has happened
To turn me into
A shadow
Of what I once was?
-shadow girl

Exit the Labyrinth

The Three Sisters

Shame is the blanket that has been stripped from your bare body. She is the cold that lingers after and refuses to leave. The feeling that someone is watching you lay there, judging your shape, your naked body. Shame is the sister of Guilt and Fear. Like Guilt, she makes you feel as if you have done something bad, something *wrong*. Guilt, her older sister, is the black sheep of the family. Everything she does has an element of secrecy to it. You know she's hiding something, even if she won't tell you the truth.

This is the difference between the two sisters. Unlike Guilt, Shame will leave you feeling exposed. She is the nightmare that you're giving a speech with a massive crowd watching your every move, and then you suddenly realize you're not wearing any clothes. Everyone is staring at you with disgust. And there you are, naked, for the entire world to see. Shivering and vulnerable. Guilt has always been known to ride her coattails, following in her sister's footsteps. But she's the gossip of the bunch. She's the one that goes around telling everyone about your mishap behind your back. She hates confrontation and will do just about anything to avoid it, even if she's tearing away at her own seams. Calling her out of it is no good either. Once you find out about it and say speak up, she dives right into a pool of tears and self-pity.

Fear is the youngest sister. She is the loner of the bunch, spending most of her time alone. They say she has a darkness to her, that she's troubled. That she spends too much time lurking in the shadows, watching over everyone else in secret. She trails behind her elder sisters, always keeping a fair distance away. Fear is the last of the light and the beginning of the dark. She appears when you flick off the lights and run up the stairs at the end of the night. She is the girl no one will hang out with. The one your mother warns you about. A girl with too many stories to tell that no one will sit down to hear.

The three sisters feed off trauma. They bask in its glory. They are creatures of the darkness and can only be warded off by light. As you experience the traumas and conflicts that come with the human experience, it is inevitable you will meet all three of the sisters. They are ancient and wise and can teach you about the world, about others, and yourself. But when they greet you, be wary. Don't let them stay past their leave, make sure they don't stay. Because once you let them in, they'll never want to go away.

Exit the Labyrinth

Shard by shard I break

Into splinters of glass

Shattered,

I collapse.

I'm running water

Disappearing through

Your fingers

Right through

The cracks

-broken

Exit the Labyrinth

Raindrops fall like tears

Onto the ground

A thousand shattered mirrors

An image refracted from itself.

Her face once so recognizable

Now disoriented

With jagged edges

A puzzle with missing pieces

But where did they go?

-whose face is this?

Exit the Labyrinth

Lord forgive me
For I have sinned
Take my body, my soul
So that I may repent.
Lay your wrath down
Your shining cross of a sword
Slay me
A beast in the night
I will emerge
No longer hidden in the shadows
A beast in the light
A monster among men
I am losing this fight.

Lord forgive me
For I have sinned
Will you still accept me?
With the wrongs I committed?
For I cannot hide any longer
I must be seen.
I cannot run any farther
From this hell I am living.
Lord please save me
Bring me to your promised lands
So that I may finally rest.
My soul is in your hands.
-if there's a God, you'll put me out of my misery

Exit the Labyrinth

Darkness floods in
Thrashing against the walls
Leaving nothing alive
Except one.
Barely breathing,
Treading with hope of rescue
She sinks deeper into the water
But there's no one coming
To save her.
She is all alone.
-drowning silently

Exit the Labyrinth

Sometimes I still lay awake at night

Thinking about what they did to me in the night

It got worse when it started happening during the day

But at least in my mind I was far, far away

-*why can't I catch a break?*

Exit the Labyrinth

I wonder if you know how much it haunts me

What you did to me

Now that I've regained all of my memories.

I can still feel them in me

Spiders creeping all over my dead body

Your filthy hands that stained me.

I hate you for the wicked scenarios you made

And all of the games you made us play

Every. Single. Damn. Day.

You never hesitated

To force me to get your way.

I prayed for the day

When it would end

And live happily ever after

If I ever made it till then.

-*bad memories*

Exit the Labyrinth

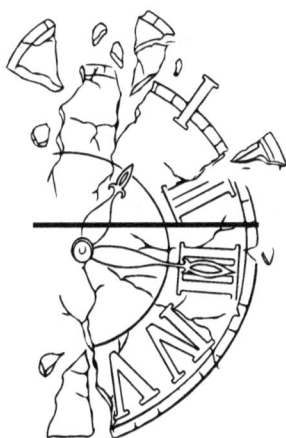

Exit the Labyrinth

You wonder why I won't speak to you
Why I went ahead and cut you off
But do you remember
What you put me through
In our shared bedroom of that house?
Make believe is a game made for children
Innocent and pure
But you just had to go ahead
And turn it into something more.
I had forgotten for so long
We even became friends
But now that I remember
Things will never be the same.
I went for so long
Burying those secrets to protect your name
When we both know
You would never do the same.
Memories haunt me
Day and night
I find myself wondering
If I'll ever live a normal life.
Hate me now,
I don't care if you do
But I'm sick and tired of pretending

Exit the Labyrinth

That things between us are still good.

Because the truth is

I'll never forgive you

For all of the fucked up shit

You put me through.

-I remember, now what?

Exit the Labyrinth

It's reached the point
Where I can't even touch myself
In mindless bliss
Because now the shadows that cloud my mind
Show me only dirty hands
Covered in blood
My pleasure is a sin
My body belongs to no one.

What kind of God are you?
And what kind of devil am I?
Do I not deserve to feel pleasure?
Why do I feel so dirty
When those hands weren't even mine?

Spoiled rotten fruit
Bruised and beaten
No one wants the baggage;
I have nothing to believe in.

What did I do to deserve this?
Do I deserve nothing?
Not an ounce of happiness?
Oh poor fucking me
Who's body I can't even touch
Even my mind is run by demons
That answer to no one.
-shame and guilt

Exit the Labyrinth

Cauldron of smoke

Pockets of gold

The evil eye watches you as you go

Tell me why you live in fear?

Is it because hell is empty

And all the devils live here?

Isn't that what Will said?

Isn't that what they show you

At night before bed?

Panic and shaken with fear

Don't you realize?

The devil is my face staring back in the mirror.

-don't keep a mirror at the end of your bed

Chapter III: Avoidance Is My New Best Friend

"Hell is empty and all the devils are here."
— William Shakespeare, The Tempest

Exit the Labyrinth

When I fell down the rabbit hole, I reached out for anything to grab to cushion the blow. More often than not, I clung to my vices for dear life. They were my only escape once my mind became a dark place. Whether it was drowning my sorrows in a bottle or in another, I was willing to do whatever I could to avoid facing my dire reality, to avoid facing what I had become. And all the while, I started to turn into a monster myself, which made me want to hide from the mirror even more. So I just kept tumbling down.

Exit the Labyrinth

You can spend your entire life running

From the parts of yourself

You're too afraid to face

But how do you make sense of the woman in the

mirror

Who seems so out of place?

-who am I?

Exit the Labyrinth

Four at night is when it starts getting dark
I see my past flash before my eyes
Through streetlights and stop signs
On the highway I'm going ninety five.
Running people off the road
I push them over the side
Or tail them all the way
Straight down '95.
Mascara tears streaming down my face
Blocking my vision
Speeding up, but I can't see
I'm swerving all over the road
Replaying the memories of you and me.
Too distorted I don't even know what's real
Was it all just a lie?
Blacked out I'm full of anger
Choking on my ego and my pride
Get home and ask myself the question:
How did I survive?
-road rage

Exit the Labyrinth

I was a winter baby
How could I not love snow?
The fresh crisp blanket of powder
Soothed the worries in my soul

It was alway more fun
When we played in it together
I was lightning
You were my thunder
Sledding down the hill
We moved so fast
Until one day
We finally crashed.

Face first we hit a brick wall
All our fun ended with pain
All that snow
Melted into slush in the rain
You were so mad at me then
I knew we'd never be the same.

The next hours were spent
Naked shaking in my bathtub alone
Trying to warm myself up
But God I was so cold

The frostbite ate me up
Until the next morning light
I felt so empty on the inside
I think a part of me died.
-*fresh cut snow*

Exit the Labyrinth

Wine red is the color of my bile

My mouth filled with sour grapes mixed with ash

I'm not sure how long I've been lying on the

bathroom floor

Or how long it will take to drag my limp body to

the cold mess of my bed.

My room mimics my life, in shambles

I'm half naked and unsure when I got undressed

Maybe that's the reason there's clothes all over

the floor

And why I seek the cold refresh of tiles

Rather than my self-built pit of hell.

-I drank too much again

Exit the Labyrinth

Fruity pink wine

Looks tempting in the bottle

So I go ahead

And pour myself a glass

Surprised that it tastes

Better than the lust that never lasts

Dancing around the room

Having conversations with my cat

Tonight will I weep

Or have a good laugh?

-*wine drunk*

Exit the Labyrinth

Cold winds are rising

Darkness encompasses the trees

A lonely soul wanders off into the woodlands

Looking for a way to feel free

-winter is coming

Exit the Labyrinth

It's been a year since I lost myself
Or at least tried to
In the warmth of another
The memories are all so vague
Thinking about them makes me shudder.
Liquor blanket wrapped around my bare chest
Rough hands on my hips
Wet lips on my neck.

I'm sick to my stomach the next morning
I thought maybe it was a lie
But vague memories in the darkness
Slowly eat at my mind.
What did I do?
And what is his name?
He's just another random stranger
Who I can't even blame.
-"I'm sorry- what was your name again?"

Exit the Labyrinth

To the rest of the world
I am a ball of energy
An orb of light
A glimmer of hope
Brightening the darkest of nights
But when I am all alone
Behind closed doors
I take off my mask
And let myself
Break right in half.

God, I am so tired
Of the weight of my chains
No one can relieve it
Or take away my pain.

I try not to let it overtake me
I try not to cry
But sometimes I can't help it
So I weep through the night.

I don't want to be strong.
I hate the burden of it all
But more than anything, I wish
That my life would be so much more than this.
-if only they could see

Exit the Labyrinth

I adore the sound

Of bass so loud

It drowns out

The sound of my thoughts.

I adore the almost company

The shadows of strangers dancing around me

That I'll forget the next morning.

I wonder if they realize

I wear shades

So that I won't be able to see

Blinded by the lights

Of the club and the streets

It's just another night out

Making new blurred memories

-going out

Exit the Labyrinth

The Humanity Switch

It's like all of a sudden I can't feel anything again.
One moment I can feel the ground, steady beneath
my feet. Only a second layer, the earth starts to
rumble and my whole body begins to shake.

The planet is hungry and ready for its next meal.

Opening up, it's ready to swallow us whole. I
fight back to gain control but the Earth has other
ideas. I crash hard into the ground, knees scraping
against the concrete. My hands are dirty with
blood. My clothes are soaked in red.

My biggest fear has come true: the sky has fallen.

I look around and see everyone I love. They're
shaking on the ground, just like me. I can see the
desperation in their eyes and I know we won't all
make it to morning. I see them slowly getting
picked off, one by one. Death's sweet kiss sucking
their soul from their lips. Taking them somewhere
they're much better off, but leaving their body
here, with the mess that is now our reality.

Exit the Labyrinth

Our world is ending and I can see it's catching fire and starting to burn. Scorching pieces of ash begin to fall from the sky. With each piece that comes down my flesh stings. I want to scream and cry and hide. But as I watch everyone fall to pieces around me, I know I can't afford that luxury. I have to stand tall and stay strong. Using every piece of strength that I've ever had in me.

I rise, knowing that if I fall, none of us will make it till morning.

So I gather my loved ones. One by one, I pick them up from their own pools of torment. I give them my hand to hold, my strength now becoming theirs. I take the weight holding them down and make it my own. I take as much of their pain as I can bear, and then some. I watch their shoulders drop, their bodies relax, as they feel the sweet relief I've always dreamed of. The sustenance I need to make it out of this whole. But there's no one coming to help me, so I brace myself as I feel the weight come on. I clench my teeth but hold on tight. I'm now on fire and grin at the world as I burn. Knowing it has to be me. That I must bear it

Exit the Labyrinth

so that others do not. I am the only one, the
chosen one. And the only way I'll be able to
survive

Is to turn it all off.

Exit the Labyrinth

I try to hold my head high

Keeping it straight and steady, I won't look away

At the devil on my shoulder

Whispering sweetly in my ear

To let go

And give in to fear.

"Don't you want to let go?"

"Just let go"

"Lose control"

"It's better that way, you know"

I try and shut him out

But I'm all alone and it's hard

Fighting for control of my body, my soul...

"Just go home and drink it off"

"You know you're more fun when you don't

stop"

"Who would even want you if you didn't take

your clothes off?"

I try and survive the day

Disassociate the hours away

I'll go home, sit by myself, and do the same

Until my only friend returns

Exit the Labyrinth

And stays until night ends.

"Close your eyes Rimu"

"Try and get some rest"

"Aren't you tired?"

"It's been days since you've slept"

"You have nothing to fear... just those memories

that brought you right here"

He stays with me for the night

Feeding intrusive thoughts to my mind

As dawn rises I finally close my eyes

And let myself slip away into the silence.

He comes less and less these days

But I know deep down

He lives in the dark space of my mind

Waiting for his time to come out.

-me, the devil, and my intrusive thoughts

Exit the Labyrinth

Milky white
Coursing through my veins
A rush of blood to the head
With a single flame
-a smoke

Exit the Labyrinth

I hate when they ask me about my body count
And I have to come up with a stupid lie
Because I don't want to explain
How each time I just wanted to feel alive.
You see, after they had their fun
And I pretended like I got mine
I'd curl up into a ball
Falling asleep as I cried.

No, it's not your fault that they touched me
When I was the age of five
Or that they still hadn't stopped
By the time I turned nine
And, of course, the choices I made after
Were entirely mine,
Years later I'm still drowning my sorrows
In weed and cheap wine.
Yet, I can't help but wonder
Would you have done the same
Had your shoes been mine?

So I hope you can understand
Why I feel like it's a secret I have to hide
When they shame a woman for doing
The same thing as a guy.
-*double standards*

Exit the Labyrinth

Cold and shaking

How long has it been since I slept?

I crave something —anything— that will scratch

this itch.

My stomach growls

Begging for the sweet caffeine

That is my only reprieve.

That and nicotine

Is the only sustenance I require

For my tired mind and drooping eyes.

My warriors, my heroes

Fighting off the nightmares that will eat me alive

If I let down my guard for a second

And face the wrath of shutting my eyes

-*hungover*

Chapter IV: Almost Love; Falling

"It is a far, far better thing that I do, than I have ever done; it is a far, far better rest that I go to than I have ever known"
— Charles Dickens, A Tale of Two Cities

Exit the Labyrinth

No matter our past, it's human nature to crave love. Yearning to be cared for by another, to feel *close*. When we experience trauma, it wears down the soul leaving the heart heavy. Afterward, there remains a stain. and no one ever wants to pick the bruised fruit.

Yet whether we can help it or not, we find ourselves falling time and time again. Whether it be for a pair of sparkling eyes or a coy smile, at the end of the day it's in our nature to form connections. The issue with having unhealed trauma and having feelings at the same time is that it leads to having toxic and unhealthy relationships. We end up searching for something in another that we lack in ourselves, giving when we have nothing left. Taking bits of each other's souls and leaving less scraps for the next.

We continue dancing between the same cycles, relearning the same lessons until the day that one person comes along and breaks your heart so deeply, you wonder if you'll ever piece it back together again. Until your ego has been so battered and bruised, leaving you so broken you believe that you're incapable of love. The chaos inside of yourself finally caught up with your relationship, and you're left to deal with it all on your own.

Each time I've fallen it's been different and yet the same. The same person with a new name. So these next two chapters are for you, or at least the many different versions I've met of you.

Exit the Labyrinth

As the leaves change

So do we

And I can't help but wonder

If you'll leave too

-*autumn isn't supposed to be blue*

Exit the Labyrinth

Will you love me and never leave?
Or will my heart turn cold and barren
When the leaves fall from the trees?
-where will the winter take us?

Exit the Labyrinth

Tell me what it is I have to do
I'm willing to do whatever it takes
Just to get close to you
For you, you see I am a fool
You are the prize
I cannot lose
-if I can't have you, no one should

Exit the Labyrinth

Static
We're electricity
You and me.
I'm the light in your dark
It's like we were meant to be.

Don't you dare tell me
Short circuits burn down
That you and me
Will never work out,
We won't die that easily.

Even though your temper's worsened
And you drive me crazy
It's you and me until the end
Or at least it ought to be.
-the perfect storm

Exit the Labyrinth

I have no greater desire
Than to be scorched by your holy fire
I have never been closer to the heavens
Than when I am alone with you
-heaven is here with you

Exit the Labyrinth

The sunrise today

Brings a dawn like no other

Rays of golden light

Shining out on the open road

A path

A future

Ignites in my eyes

Lying right there in front of me

Next to you

-sunrise

Exit the Labyrinth

In my mind I'm consumed by oranges and blues

Rose colored glasses

My heart turns pink for you

Vibrant hues paint the skies and the river too

Running through sunsets

Finding my way back to you

-rose colored glasses

Exit the Labyrinth

Exit the Labyrinth

When I sit on the beach
I can't help but think of you and me
Those midsummer nights spent on the shore
Gazing at the sea wishing we'd be more
-wishing while watching the waves

Exit the Labyrinth

As I watch the ripples of the tide

I can't help but wish you were here by my side

Taking in this magnificent view

Your eyes looking back at me

The same blue

-ocean eyes and ocean tides

Exit the Labyrinth

I've lost all sense of how the earth spins on its
axis
There is no difference between the past, future,
and present
There is only here
Only now
Just me and your lips, somehow
-x and y, me and you

Exit the Labyrinth

Galaxies swirl through my mind

A place beyond space and time

How is it that I have traveled past the moon

Without leaving this very room?

-my mars is in pisces

Exit the Labyrinth

How Badly I Wanted You

I long to get under your sheets, under your clothes, under your skin. I want to feel you all over and breathe you in deep. Every inch of you until I can take no more. If only for a moment, I want it to feel like we have forever. That stars will burn before I have to yearn for you again. I want you to make me feel something —something so close to being real that I can nearly taste it on my lips. I want you to make me feel like there's more out there than just us. Greater beings and energies that led us right into each other's arms. I want you to hold me close, so close I can't breathe. I want to lay with you and simply exist. Arms and legs tangled in a bed too small to fit the both of us.

I want you to make me feel alive, an animal filled with rage and passion that cannot be contained. I want to fall asleep with you, our minds floating into the great unknown. I want to wake up with you, gazing deeply into your sleepy eyes as I roll over. I want you to pull me in close, your favorite blanket, when you just need someone to be there. I want to know you, your deepest desires, the fears that keep you up at night. I want you all to myself, leaving nothing at all, ever, for anyone else. I want you to give your all to me, your mind, body, and soul. I want you to crave me as much as I crave you. Because there's nothing more in this entire world that I want right now as badly as I want you.

Exit the Labyrinth

When we touch

Our hearts turn into fire

Souls engulfed in flames

Maybe one of these days we'll both let our walls

down

And watch the world burn beneath us

-*sex on fire*

Exit the Labyrinth

I crave you

As the moon yearns for the sun

Orbiting around the planet

Until the day comes

When we can finally unite

And become one

-I guess it's true that I crave you

Exit the Labyrinth

Golden drops of sunshine drip from her skin

Her smile lights up like the sun from above

With a chuckle, she knocks her head back, toasty

brown eyes squinting shut

Copper strands of hair mingling across the grass

and flowers

A goddess before you, she glows in the light

Skin as soft as cocoa butter

You want more as she reaches out

You touch under the sun

Your bodies connected, your hearts beating as one

You and her

Your golden girl

-*golden girl*

Exit the Labyrinth

Your haunted eyes follow me into the dark

Shadows dancing in the rain

As the moon eclipses us

Our bodies connect

Souls tango into the abyss

Of who we are versus what we know

-haunted love

Exit the Labyrinth

Sunset hues

Meshed with winter blues

A fleeting feeling

Lingering thoughts in a breeze

I wonder how often

You think of me

-before the seasons change

Chapter V: The Many Versions of You; Crashing

This love I feel, that feel no love in this
—William Shakespere, Romeo and Juliet

Exit the Labyrinth

As months go by
I see you less and less
But the taste of your skin
Still remains on my lips.

-lips that linger

Exit the Labyrinth

It's been so long since I've seen your face

You look so different

And yet feel the same

I can't help but wonder

How much you've changed

-who are you now?

Exit the Labyrinth

Before I knew it

I was falling again

Another pair of twinkly blue eyes

That held my stare.

If there's anything I know to be true

It's that I could never get sick of that hue

Or the many different versions I've met of you

-the many versions I've met of you

Exit the Labyrinth

Even if I wanted to

I know that I could not

For what we had is dead and gone.

I've seen this story before

We both know how it ends

There is no universe that exists

Where we could just be friends.

-it was never just casual between us

Exit the Labyrinth

If I think too hard I'll cry
So I just leave my mind blank most of the time.

I sit watch as the seasons go by
It's fucking depressing without you by my side
-another sad and lonely winter

Exit the Labyrinth

Though I may try

I cannot explain the pain

Of being in your presence

So vividly in my dreams again.

Has it been so long?

Since I grazed your skin, your lips

Been privy to your touch

Felt you deep beyond my hips.

I woke up burning

With a desire I hadn't felt in forever

But when I tried to fall back asleep

I knew you were long gone.

-I long for sweet dreams, but you are my favorite
nightmare

Exit the Labyrinth

You painted your room from orange to green

You rearranged your belongings and forgot about

me

You whispered sweet lies into my ear

And only spoke words I never wanted to hear

I've been broken now for over a year

I'm still trapped in your cage

Still frozen in fear

I find myself still crying in the night

Empty except for the hate you left behind.

-something in the evergreen

Exit the Labyrinth

It is taking all of my effort

Just to stay away

From the way you feel

While mouthing my name

-those lips I miss

Exit the Labyrinth

I missed being rocked

By your melancholy lullaby

Into a sweet slumber

The only place

Where we will meet again.

-I'd sleep forever if it meant being with you

Exit the Labyrinth

Endings and beginnings

Leave my heart in woe

How do I make sense of these feelings

When you left me out in the cold?

-alone again

Exit the Labyrinth

I thought we would have spoken by now
Funny to me how I still haven't figured you out
The nights grow longer and colder
How I yearn for things to go back to what they
could have been.

We were never really together
And yet we were so close to having it all
Right before the crash and the fall.

They say a fire that burns too bright isn't meant to
last
Guess it makes sense as to why I was never yours.
-lighting fires for fun

Exit the Labyrinth

You break me down

Push and shove

I'm a bloody mess

On the ground

Heart heavy

Head pounding

A thousand dead butterflies

Floating in my stomach

Where did the lust go?

The almost love

All the feelings

I thought I knew

Dead and gone

As I turn black and blue

-fight club

Exit the Labyrinth

If I am ever granted the honor

To gaze upon your face

Even if it is just for a second

Or in a momentary haste

Even if it's just in my slumber

With so many unspoken syllables between us two

Know that I will cherish it

Until I bleed true

-will we ever meet again?

Exit the Labyrinth

Heart of gold and a mind of fire

What are her truest desires?

A burning passion

An endless flame

A deep voice echoing the sound of her name

In her dreamscape one night he came

Her knight in shining armor

To rescue the princess stuck in the tower.

He almost succeeded

Almost brought her down

But then he decided

To leave her up there

While he stayed on the ground

So she laid there

Burning a hole with her screams

There was no one to save her

Not even in her dreams.

-the princess in the tower

Exit the Labyrinth

The Birds, Beetles, and Butterflies

When disaster strikes, it's the insects and small animals that first take flight. The birds, the beetles, and the butterflies. All other animals follow. They say elephants can sense unfamiliar movement from hundreds of miles away. When they're being attacked, they signal other elephants by sending out abnormal movement patterns they can sense through echoing vibrations in the earth. Humans feel different sensations in the body, hairs rising up the back of our necks or an intuitive gut feeling. If only I knew the fluttering feeling in my stomach was a warning sign.

Excitement and anxiety are the same emotion on two different ends of the spectrum. Excitement is light and bubbly, it screams happiness. Anxiety is silently screaming. How easy it is to mistake the two. Every sensation in your body is heightened as you feel the pitter patter of millions of wings thrashing against the walls of your stomach, fighting for a way out. You can feel the adrenaline rushing like heroin to the bloodstream, intoxicating every inch of your being. That's what it felt like to be in your

110

presence. Only I could not distinguish the bad from the good.

In hindsight, your vision is always 20/20, but when you're so deep into the moment, you never know whether you're making the right choice. You just act instinctively. Will your body stay and fight, or does it scream and flight? I should've picked the latter when it came to you. But instead I stayed. Much longer than I should have, too. If only I had known better then…

Exit the Labyrinth

I tell myself I should've known better
Than to fall for those gleaming eyes
You seemed so perfect at the start
Ripping wings off butterflies so that I could see
them.
I looked at you like you had the world
And just like that you were willing to give me
some of yours.
A taste was enough for me
Your words were just so sweet
Sugar coated, handpicked just for me
How could I not believe every pretty lie?
I can still hear your voice
Soft as morning rain
Coaxing dark thoughts
That rot in my brain.
Your energy is poison
Spreading to every flower in the garden
Devouring everything it touches.

I should've known better
Than to enter your chamber of secrets
Without sacrificing my own.
I gave myself to you completely

Exit the Labyrinth

Chopping off my hand so that you would have

one to hold

Holding it tightly so that yours wouldn't get cold

Little did I know that you already had many more.

Another trophy on the shelf

A medal added to the collection

I was just another girl

That meant nothing in your world

A soon to be distant memory

A diluted dream

That I wouldn't be

Had I known better

- *I should've known*

Exit the Labyrinth

I tried to give you the world

In the palm of my hand

But instead of cherishing the planet

Which I had handcrafted specially for you

You took it

And crushed it

A bug beneath your shoe

And just like that

My whole world disappeared

And you were gone with it.

-but you! you were my whole world!

Exit the Labyrinth

The sun creeps out again

Diminishing all the darkness dusk brought in

Two twin souls, I fell in love in the twilight

There I sat and watched you glow

As I got swept away, taken by the shadows.

If you had asked

I would've stayed

And let the night take my light away

But you didn't, anyway.

Still, I stayed and waited

But dawn didn't break

And the day never came.

I was lost then

A lonely wandering soul

Creating chaos to fill the void

Drinking to keep me whole

Wasting away my life

Waiting for you to come home.

In the darkness I saw a patch of light

A silhouette came to guide me through the night

They give the man many names

But to me he is always the same

Exit the Labyrinth

Holy and mighty, they call him God

Masculine or feminine, he is both, he is all

With a breath of fresh air he told me trust him

To let go and freefall

I tried to cling on for dear life

But there was nothing to cling to

You left me behind

Silently, I wished you one last goodbye

Knowing I was leaving your cave

For the last time.

-the exitway

Exit the Labyrinth

Bittersweet

Is this end

That I feared was coming?

As dark turns to light

We finally say our goodbyes.

In my heart was your fire

A deep burning desire

That is now long gone

Off it travels

Whispering away with the wind

To a far off land

I would never see again.

-another goodbye

Exit the Labyrinth

Exit the Labyrinth

I'm not sure which is worse

Knowing that you're gone for good

Or that one day

You'll be coming home to another

-my loss is their gain

Exit the Labyrinth

I spent one year getting over you
Because at first it was just a t-shirt that you kept
between us
But each time I saw you, the silence between us
grew.

I should have known
By the way you never looked me in the eyes
That it was too good to be true
A delusion made up in my mind
But when we kissed
It felt like time did not exist
All that I thought I knew
Was me and you
-was it even real?

Exit the Labyrinth

Rich maroon

Always tastes better split between two

But you left

And in my now lonesome home

I sip on melancholy memories

Of what could have been.

Until I see flames in the horizon

And I fade with the darkness

I look forward to the next day

Where I do it all again

-it should be me and you, but all I have left is this

bottle

Exit the Labyrinth

Scorching heat

Fuming like the pits of hell

I burn for you no longer

And instead wish to watch you

Catch fire

And go up in flames

I guess you could call it anger

But I prefer female rage

-hell hath no fury like a woman scorned

Exit the Labyrinth

I swear

This is the last time

I'll stay up this late

And let my mind wander

Back into your imaginary arms

That I beg to told me tighter

Than you ever did

-I no longer yearn for you

Exit the Labyrinth

The Other Woman

I find that the hardest part of dealing with relationships that took a turn for the worst are the triggers. They say that anything can be a trigger. My blood begins to boil every time I see a girl that even *slightly* resembles her. There I am, sitting at work, cheeks beginning to blush, my vision transforming into a deep scarlet red. My internal temperature rises until I can feel the fire taking over from inside of me: I begin to burn in my seat. The other woman. That's all I ever was, all I've ever been. Time and time again, never chosen by the man that I loved. Always the runner up, never first place. *What does she have that I don't?* What could it be other than my personality, the thing that makes me, *me*?

I can't say that I've ever fully gotten over my petty jealousies, although I am working on it. I don't beat myself over it either because I know it's all a part of the healing process. I can't say that I haven't stalked her page a billion times. I can't say that I've seen pictures of them together and haven't died a little on the inside. Time and time again, it's the same broken record spinning around in circles. And yet it never gets any easier. You see, all of my romantic relationships have ended the same. With a new version of him picking the girl that was a better option than me. The good girl, a simple choice for them. They will always choose the person that they don't have to worry about. The person that wasn't me.

Maybe I was too much to handle. Just a bit too messy, I was the wild card. Completely unpredictable, I was never worth the gamble of their hearts. I was the "fun" girl that you kept around for a short time, never a long time. The perfect friends with benefits, the ideal sneaky link. The one you hide from your family but brag about to your friends. The one that afterwards, you'll never speak about again. You ghost me and, eventually, I turn into a distant memory. Each and every single time, it ends the same.

I think they usually regret it, at least a little. Years later you think they would've made some changes to their lives, but they never do. Some try to come back but they all lurk in the shadows, watching from afar, wondering how differently their lives would've played out had they chosen differently. I guess the grass always looks greener on the other side. And while their path led them between the legs of another, my path led me back down the road to myself.

It's funny how no matter what you choose, the loss of one love leads you to gain a new one. Each time I bounce back faster and learn to love myself a little bit deeper. After months or even years of mourning them and what we could have been, I begin to see the situation for what it truly is, rather than through my glasses tainted with heartbreak. They didn't choose me and therefore will never deserve me. That's what always brings me back. They abandoned me. Left me out in the cold. The girl that you never chose is someone you now will never get to know. The door that was left cracked open for so long closes so that a new one can open. The one back to myself. And though I was the other woman for him, he would've never been the right man for me either.

Exit the Labyrinth

It's not you that I miss

Not the late nights spent sneaking around

Not the rough sex

Not your icy hands intertwined around my neck.

Not the hours spent in silence

Or whispers of sweet nothings

Not you at all, in fact

All along I've been missing something I've never
even had

The same thing I've been searching for in every
version of you I've ever met:

Myself.

-it was never you, it was always me

The Veil

Exit the Labyrinth

There is only a thin veil that separates us from living in the dark rather than the light. The veil is what keeps us in the shadows, wandering aimlessly around the labyrinth. Only once we remove the blanket can we begin to navigate the way out. In order to remove the veil we must make a decision: the decision to truly *try*. The only thing harder than surviving is finding a reason to survive. But only when we make that conscious decision do we see any forward movement. We must decide that we deserve better. We must choose more for ourselves.

Like anything in life, the only way to make a change is to truly begin. You have to decide, to realize that you are worth it. That you are worth all of the effort you put into yourself. That you deserve better, you deserve *more*. Life isn't made to be spent in misery. Yes, things got bad. Terrifying and traumatizing. And it is going to take time, a whole lot of it, to get better. But things can change if you're willing to put in the work.

You must change in order for the world around you to change. The world will shift with you, but fluidity is required. Whether or not you live the rest of your existence in the darkness is completely up to you. Not everyone makes it to the light, the other side. The dark can and will swallow you whole, but only if you let it.

Remember —a labyrinth is not linear. The path does not lead straight out. However, It is not a maze either. There are no dead ends. There are no walls. It is continuous, and you can easily spend your entire lifetime adrift its paths, wandering in circles. Or you can put your fear aside and continue the path forward, the path out.

I spent so much of my life wasted in the darkness. Years and moments I will never get back. As much as I would like, I think if given the chance, I wouldn't take it back. I would do everything (or at least most things) exactly the same. Because here I am, and things finally seem…better. But not until the day I decided that I finally had enough.

I was at my breaking point when I decided to make a change. After many years spent in misery, I finally hit the bottom of the abyss: rock bottom. I had nothing, I had become nothing. I hated myself more than I ever had before. I couldn't look at my image in the mirror, at the monster I had become. The shell of all my hopes and dreams. Everything I ever wanted for myself, everything I desired became a distant memory. The paper tower I had spent my entire life building came crashing down. My career was failing. All the people that meant anything to me had left me alone in the cold. And I was just existing. Waiting for the other shoe to drop. Waiting for the sweet death I yearned for.

Every day was hell. I was going through the motions trying to keep myself alive. I had truly hit the bottom of the well. I spent years circling around this grey area until I got to this point. I realized this is all my life was ever going to be. A sad tale about a girl that was once a dreamer. A girl that once had hope until life snatched it away from her, and left her with nothing.

It was at that very point that I had enough. I was fucking done. So over my shitty life and my shitty self. I was sick and tired of hating myself. Hating my life. Hating everyone who had left me alone to rot in it. I was just so tired. Living had become a chore. Nothing was good, and everything that had once been beautiful turned out to be just as doomed as I was. I spent so many nights begging the heavens and the skies for some type of reprieve. But I did not get any, not until I decided that I deserved it. That I *deserved* better. That's when the veil was removed.

I deserved to live. I deserved to *want* to live. It wasn't fair that there were people in the world that woke up every day and did not want to exist. It wasn't fair that I was one of them. I deserved to wake up and feel happy, or at least feel like the sky wasn't going to come crashing down on me. It was at this point that I started to realize I wanted more for myself. That I was worth it. And that whatever it took to get there would perhaps be worth it too.

There were no guarantees about what the other side of it would look like. But at this point, I saw that I had no other choice. I could either spend the rest of my existence continuing to go through the motions and praying for the day when it would finally be over. Turn around and repeat the same cycles that would lead me back here, to this very spot or somewhere even worse. I could either call it quits now and go back, or I could muster up all the courage I had left in me and fight. Fight like my life depended on it, because it truly did. Fight for a chance at life worth living.

And I decided that it was at least worth a shot. In truth I had nothing better to do. Everything was dark and gray and stormy and I just couldn't take it anymore. Something had to change. *I* had to change. So I decided to give it my all, or at least whatever I had left to give. And I did.

I tried. Tried as best and as hard as I could. I fought to live.

I started to truly tune into the signs the universe was giving me. That was when the memories from my past started flooding back. Everything brought back memories, everything became a trigger. I slowly realized that the world I was living in was one I could no longer belong to, not if I was going to become the version of myself I was meant to be: my true self, my healed self. That the price for the life I wanted, the life that I was being led to, was my old one. I was going to have to burn my entire life to the ground and start over from scratch.

Chapter VI : Detachment (The In-Between)

"I'm Nobody! Who are you?"
— Emily Dickinson

Exit the Labyrinth

It can be quite a scary feeling to be neither here nor there. A part of you has died and yet the new version of yourself hasn't quite set in yet. Your new skin isn't as comfortable as the old, and each time you try on the one you've shedded you realize it's outgrown you. You are in the inbetween. Everything around you is changing. You find yourself unable to fit in the same environments you once did. Familiar faces turn into strangers, and though you can finally recognize the reflection in the mirror, it seems as if no one else does.

The inbetween is represented by the element of change. You are no longer the person you've been, and your life begins to reflect the new and improved version of yourself. It is common to struggle with detaching from the past —people, places, habits— but that takes time. As you finally become whole within yourself, you begin to realize that you no longer require the same vices you once used to patch up the parts of you that were missing. What worked for the old version for yourself isn't going to work for the new. You've changed. Now it's time for your world to change with it.

Detachment is rooted in letting go. It is time for you to let go of everything that was attached to the old version of yourself. That means quitting the job that makes you miserable and doesn't pay you enough. No longer spending time with people that don't want better for you or themselves, even if you've known them your entire life. This part is difficult and requires you to start spending more time alone than ever. You may even feel as if you no longer have a place in the world around you, and the truth is that you don't.

You are between two timelines —the past and the future. And you can no longer stay where you once were, not if you truly want to make a change in your life. The change you desire requires sacrifice. It requires sacrificing everything you've ever known and letting your entire life burn to the ground so you can start over again. Only then can you plant new seeds. And still it will be a while before you can harvest the fruit.

Exit the Labyrinth

It is going to take time to get your dream job or opportunity that uproots your life to the city you've always dreamed of living in. Or to make new friends who are just as motivated as you to accomplish their goals. And if this means you have to spend some time alone, then so be it. You are better off alone than in the company of those who will hold you back. You are your decisions —how you choose to act, what you choose to do with your time, and who you choose to spend it with. Your entire world is a reflection of you. And while you reshape who you are, you must accept that in order to become your dream version of yourself, you have to let go of everything which no longer fits that image.

So you let go. You go into hermit mode and start working on yourself. You visualize how you want this new version of yourself to be, how you wish to present yourself to the world and those around you. You work on yourself and wait. No matter how long it takes to see results. No matter how long it takes for your manifestations to come in. You must keep working on yourself until you truly feel like the version of yourself you've always wanted to become.

Remember, there are two different ways you can experience the inbetween, though you'll probably do both. The inbetween can either be the bus you're waiting for that just won't come or some extra time that you get to spend outside. You can spend this time caught up in how cold it is, or how the evening sky is taking over. How you'd rather be anywhere else then where you are right now. Or you can enjoy the fresh air. Listen to the sounds of the birds chirping to one another, or maybe have a conversation with a mysterious stranger. The Inbetween is what you make it. No matter how you choose to spend this time, the bus isn't going to come any faster, so you might as well enjoy whichever parts of it you can. Because when the bus finally comes, you'll be speeding away wishing that you took the time to relax while you still had the chance.

Exit the Labyrinth

Needle in a haystack

Intermission or interlude

I'm not sure where I'm going

But I need a new view

Stuck in the inbetween

Of space and time

How can I find the exit

In the labyrinth of my mind?

-the in-between

Exit the Labyrinth

Dancing in the nether realm

Not here nor there

Somewhere in between

Both somewhere nowhere.

Not at peace but not in fear

Shadows of who I've left

And who's coming near.

For now I suppose I'll travel

This journey by myself

Floating through the ether

With nothing left of my old self.

-free fall

Exit the Labyrinth

Drifting from my past

The person I once was

Seems so distant now

And the person I'm becoming

Still seems so far away

But here I am

Stuck in the middle

Floating around

With one question on my mind:

Where do I go from here?

-*stuck in the middle*

Exit the Labyrinth

I have grown so much and yet I am still the same
Sitting on the porch of my big blue house
Listening to ghosts scream my name
-big blue house

Exit the Labyrinth

The Waiting Game

It is a natural reaction to have your blood pressure rise as you watch good things happen to the people who hurt you the most. It's normal to feel your blood boil over having to see them gain praise or recognition, knowing that others will never see their true colors or understand the hurt they caused you. It stings even more when you're down in the dumps, still bitter and hurting. You're left feeling betrayed while they go on without a care in the world. That's when the rage takes over, turning you into the green eyed monster you never thought you'd become. But then again, you never thought they would do those things to you either.

As we age, we begin to realize just how many shades of gray there are in this world. For the most part, no one is truly evil, just as no one is completely good. We have all done right and done wrong to some extent. So, who is to decide what we deserve from this world?

The answer is simple to understand, yet hard to accept: it's not up to you to. The laws of the universe demand balance, and karma eventually comes to collect its dues. The hard part is the waiting period. We must remember that our blessings are still on their way to us. What others have now does not affect what we have coming. The blessings that are meant for us are for us only. No one can take what's rightfully yours, *divinely* yours. It may take a little more time, but some things are worth the wait. And what's coming to those of us that have silently suffered through our battles, have kept our heads high when everything and everyone in our lives has tried to tear us down, who still break out a smile or crack a joke to make others laugh on our darkest days, is worth waiting for.

And when the day comes that *they* are the ones sitting on the sidelines, watching *you* rise like a phoenix from the ashes, *that* is the day you receive your justice. Your justice is them watching you live the life of your dreams and never getting to be a part of it.

Exit the Labyrinth

My sage lights a fire

Burning down my old home

I intended to clear the darkness away

But instead the flames engulfed

Filling the house with smoke.

You would think I'd sit and choke

But my lungs have seen far worse

My kittens sit there with me patiently

They'd never leave my side

Familiar like a glass of old cherry wine.

So I stand outside and watch it burn

Sipping on the sweet innocence

I lost in that very place

Replacing it with something new.

Ash- it fertilizes the land of my new garden

Sage now mixed with smoke and dirt

Burying my old burdens

The house was never a home.

-burn a house, build a garden

Chapter VII: Change

"Yet knowing how way leads on to way,
I doubted if I should ever come back."
— Robert Frost, The Road Not Taken

Exit the Labyrinth

The dark dank walls of the labyrinth transform as they begin to reflect a glowing light that was nonexistent in its depths. With each step you take forward, it gets brighter. You cannot hide the smile on your face as you settle into the knowing that after all this time and hard work, you're nearly there. That you can now finally see the light. You're finally almost out.

This is the part where the biggest change happens: the one inside of you. The world you spent your entire life building has burned to the ground. Everything is different now. You've been working so hard for a new beginning. But there is still one thing that keeps holding you back. It is the hardest part of this journey, the part that takes the longest, and is the key to transforming into the version of yourself you've always dreamed of: healing. True, deep healing of your worst traumas.

Up until this point, I'd spent my entire life running from my past. Pretending like nothing bad had ever happened to me. Pretending like I, and everything around me, was okay. Because if I didn't —if I let those memories in my mind— I would have to face the truth: that things weren't okay. *I* wasn't okay.

We aren't born toxic and miserable. We don't inherit being hateful of the world and distrusting everyone who wants a place in our lives. We are made this way by our experiences. All of the negative talk from those around you. The cruel actions others have taken against you. All of the sadness, all of the hurt adds up and transforms us into something we are not. If we do not have the tools and resources to deal with these experiences in a healthy way, we develop unhealthy coping mechanisms. We let them guide us down the slippery slope downward into the abyss.

You cannot exit the labyrinth of your mind without dealing with your trauma. There is no way around it. You must undergo the healing process and fully submit yourself to the healing journey. Whatever it was that happened to you, you must learn to accept it. Accept it happened. Accept it was awful and you didn't deserve it. Validate yourself for feeling angry and upset and hateful. Accept that you didn't want to accept what happened, and that's what led you here. This part isn't easy. It's time consuming and more often than not, seems impossible. Often, this is the stage where we must ask for assistance, which is a feat in itself. But this is also the part where you must accept that you need help.

So get help. Ask. Scream. Yell. Do whatever it takes, exhaust every resource. But you cannot move forward with the healing journey until you come into acceptance. And once you have fully come into acceptance, then you can start to feel all of the emotions you've been holding back your entire life. Let them wash over you, let yourself feel every bit of it. Bottling them up as you have for so long only feeds the darkness. The rage fuels it and the sadness leads you into the vices you used to try to escape it.

There's no more running. There's no more hiding. You must face the monster in the mirror without looking away from it. You've worked so hard. You're doing better than you ever have. But you have to keep going without looking back. Even if it is the easier option to fall back into your old ways. You must sit in discomfort. Sit until it begins to feel comfortable, and then sit a bit longer. We sit until we can face the monster that's been hiding under the bed.

I spent so much of my life feeling like I was tainted —turned into damaged goods by the things that happened to me. I thought it was something that would haunt me my entire life. I would never make it to the other side of that because what happened was so mortifying. That my wounds were too deep to heal. And how I dealt with them only made it worse. I only ever focused on how what happened traumatized me, how it left me hopeless and depressed, took away my will to live. As I began to turn my life around — letting go of toxic habits and facing my trauma — all I could think about was how gruesome it had been. And for the longest time, that's all I thought it could be.

But then I had a breakthrough: if you only focus on the negative aspects of what happened, you will never be able to release the anger that has been building inside. You must make peace with your past. The truth is, what happened to me will always stay with me —I can't erase it. And the same goes for you. You can't change what has happened or make it vanish from your memories. But how you choose to let it impact you is completely up to you.

Detachment isn't just about letting go of everything that no longer serves you, it's also about letting go of the pain and the sadness that you have been carrying on for too long. It's about making peace with what happened. Not for the sake of others, but for ourselves. So we can finally change the story.

It's time to truly move on from what happened and to let it all go. What happened to you is not the entirety of your story. It was only the beginning. You have so much more to live for, so much you can offer to the world. No matter what hardship you've faced, no matter what you've had to survive, you can come out of it and live a life of peace. That's how we begin the process of metamorphosis, how we come out of the darkness and into the light. *That's* what it means to exit the labyrinth.

No matter how difficult, how impossible it may seem, there is nothing you cannot endure if you do not give up hope. There is nothing you cannot overcome if you are willing to fight for a better life, if you are willing to at least *try*. And that's exactly what I did.

Exit the Labyrinth

In the darkest of the night skies
I watch as the sun rises
A golden ball of fire
Breaking up the mass of grey
That hid the power of the moon
It is the light of God
Vishnu or Christ
He has many names
Each avatar different
And yet all the same.
Mother Gaia, do you hear my prayers?
Do you hear my screams?
Will you help me face my fears?
Will you help me gain my strength?
And face the trauma that held me back
For all these years?
You answer
But not in tongues
Rather synchronicities
Like a bird or the sun
I am uplifted as your light shines
White light purity
The most divine
Even in the most difficult of times

Exit the Labyrinth

You've never once left my side

Guiding me throughout this life

And beyond the axis

Of space and time.

-Gods of the Universe

Exit the Labyrinth

I guess this phase is over
I guess I've truly changed
The girl I was is gone
She lived her life in vain.
Instead I've turned into a woman
One that's proud of her name
A magician, an alchemist
Transmuting beauty from pain.
-*brand new me*

Exit the Labyrinth

I used to love

The hellfire that engulfed us

Each time we touched

But you left

Your hands replaced by those of the gods

And the thought

Of being touched by another

Now scorns my soul

Only when the day comes

That I find Heaven in them

Will I strip my silken clothes

And bare open my legs

Giving birth to a new love

-the hands of God

Exit the Labyrinth

Exit the Labyrinth

I used to scream at the sky

And cry to the gods

"If you truly exist

why would you do this?"

It never made sense to me

What I did to deserve any of it

All of the pain and torture

That no child should ever have to endure...

"Why me?" was always the question

Many years later

I finally received my answer.

Though I've always had what it takes

To overcome anything

I needed some time

To fall on my face

I needed to learn and grow

And make my own mistakes

So that I understood how easy it was

To fall from grace.

The gods knew

They had to take a step back

Give me room to find my own way

Exit the Labyrinth

Whilst watching over me.

Guide me when it was needed

But let me take the lead

I had to make my own way

To get to where I needed to be.

You see

The tragedies I faced

Were the beginning of my journey

I had to overcome my fears

To share with you all, my story.

-from darkness to light

Exit the Labyrinth

Take me to the beach
Anywhere I can see the ocean and the sky
Bask in the light
Move freely, dance.

Take me to the forest
And let me gaze into the night
I am guided by the moon
Its power gives me life.

I am fueled when I step out in nature
Yet grounded by the dirt
Solid under my feet
That connects me to the Earth.

Hold me as I wake from my night terrors
Cradle me until I fall back asleep
Lay with me so we can both have
Sweet and safe dreams.

Encourage me to write
To follow my own path
Tell me I'm in control
Of how I want to live my life.

Teach me how important it is
To share my story with the world
Promise me one day it will all get better
That I'll be happy before I turn old.

Exit the Labyrinth

Make sure I use my voice as much as I can

That I stand my ground and speak my truth

And not be duped by any person or man.

Teach me how to respect by body

Make sure I understand

It's not for everybody.

Teach me my mother tongue

Make sure I speak my own language

Make sure it's ingrained in my brain

So that I can teach my future family.

Most importantly, teach me how to love myself

So that I can grow to love others

And be the best version of myself.

-teach me how

Exit the Labyrinth

Wings, oh wings, they are on fire!
Change is my heart's truest desire
A name, a face, a place I transpire
My heart aches, my body's tired
If I said I was content I would be a liar
Until the day things are different
I will continue to aspire
-change is coming

Exit the Labyrinth

When the storm clouds are the darkest
And it seems like there is nowhere to go
Know that there is a path clearing
That will lead you back home
-where I'm heading

Exit the Labyrinth

I cry and I cry
I'm not exactly sure why
But if I had to take a guess
I'd say it's because I no longer want to die
That feeling replaced
With burning desire
The joy of being alive
-it's so strange! Wanting to live!

Exit the Labyrinth

Epilogue

Though this book is coming to an end, your journey will continue on. The path forward is simply onwards. As the seasons change, so will you and the world around you. Life will continue to surprise you, throwing in curve balls whenever it can. There is only one thing that is certain in life, and that is change. Healing isn't linear, and this journey will continue on, changing and growing as you do. You will continue to find new ways to heal and more to heal from. The stability you seek will always be inside of yourself, there to tap into whenever you find yourself lacking it in the outside world.

Be proud of yourself and all of the work you have done. The worst days are over, they are now behind you. You are not the same person you once were, and you will never be that person again. Though you will continue to grow and break and grow again, one thing is certain: once you return to the light, you must never go back into the darkness again. Life wasn't built to be easy, but it isn't meant to be so hard either. As long as the light inside of you keeps shining, the world around you will never go dark again.

The hardest part is over, but where you choose to go from here is entirely up to you. You are the creator of your own reality. You have what it takes. All of the tools you need to get to where you want to go are either already within you, or will be easily accessible to you as long as you keep dreaming and believing. As long as you have faith in your journey and yourself.

That is the only way to finish this portion of your healing journey: to have true, unfaltering faith. Faith that you didn't do all of that work for nothing. Faith that your hard work will eventually pay off. Truly believing that things are better and are going to continue getting better. And most importantly, that it will never be as bad as it once was. No matter what comes next, you are a better version of yourself. You have what it takes to deal with anything else life throws at you, no matter how difficult it may seem. Everything you experience is to help you learn and grow.

Remember —things are happening *for* you, not *to* you.

As you begin to navigate what this new world will look like, what this new *you* will look like, remember to keep checking in with that version of yourself that lives inside of you. The same little girls and boys that held in their truth for so long. Remember to give them flowers every once in a while. Give them the love and care they never had. The love you've always deserved.

I, once so drained of life, now feel more alive than ever. I truly feel at ease. Comfortable. Some days are harder than others, but the light inside of me burns bright and steady. My mind, once so at war with itself, has now become a quiet, safe space. And as for the little girl inside of me —well, she hardly even screams these days.

www.ingramcontent.com/pod-product-compliance
Lightning Source LLC
Chambersburg PA
CBHW072348090426
42741CB00012B/2964